HOW TO MAKE $1000 PER DAY

AMAZON TO EBAY DROPSHIPPING

NO EXPERIENCE REQUIRED

Copyrighted Material

Copyright © 2025 - All rights reserved.

No part of this publication may be reproduced, distributed, or transmitted in any form or by any means, including photocopying, recording, or other electronic or mechanical methods, without the prior written permission of the author, except in the case of brief quotations embodied in critical reviews and certain other non-commercial uses permitted by copyright law.

Author: Money Maker Publications

Dedication

This book is dedicated to every aspiring entrepreneur who was looking for a way to make a lot of money, but still scared to take the first step and make their dream come through because of the fact that they have too many tasks on their schedule and no money to do it. Are you one of the people who want to build an online business but most likely think that "I don't have the money, time, or experience for this," then this is just for you.

To those who go for them, the person who studies late into the night, and the ones who spend every weekend working hard to get what they want--may this guide be your much-needed shortcut. Your trip to the top where you gain the success you want is about to start!

DISCLAIMER

This book is designed to provide information and inspiration to readers. The author and publisher are not responsible for any outcomes resulting from the use of the ideas or opportunities presented in this book. Individual results may vary based on effort, market conditions, and other factors.

TABLE OF CONTENTS

Introduction: 1

Chapter 1: Understanding the Amazon to eBay Business Model 2

Chapter 2: Connecting Your eBay Store to Payoneer 9

Chapter 3: Cash Flow & Fund Management 14

Chapter 4: Automation Software Setup & Configuration 19

Chapter 5: Increasing Your eBay Store Limits for Higher Profits 25

Chapter 6: Shipping, Returns, and Payment Policies Setup 31

Chapter 7: Product Listing Strategies 37

Chapter 8: eBay Keyword Research 42

Chapter 9: Title Optimization for Higher Click-Through Rates 45

Chapter 10: Automating Buyer Messages to Improve Customer Experience 48

Chapter 11: Scanning Amazon DropShippers Goods in Bulk and Dropping Their Leading Items 51

Chapter 12: Copying Amazon Products in Bulk and Listing Them on eBay in Three Clicks 55

Chapter 13: (Bonus) Secret Method to Find Walmart Dropshippers in Bulk 59

Chapter 14: Updating Tracking Numbers for Orders Efficiently 64

Chapter 15: Converting AMZL Tracking Numbers to eBay-Compatible Formats.. 68

Chapter 16: One-Click Copy Buyer Name and Shipping Address to Amazon.. 72

Chapter 17: Special Method to Use eBay Ads Without Losing a Penny 76

Chapter 18: Temp Payment Holds on eBay for New Sellers (Explanation).. 80

Chapter 19: Customer Service #1 – How to Find Solutions for Client Questions (Q&A) 84

Chapter 20: Customer Service #2 – How to Handle Product Returns and Get Shipping Labels from Amazon 88

Final Thoughts & Scaling Your eBay Dropshipping Business 92

Final Words: Take Action & Keep Scaling.. 99

Introduction:

Have you ever felt amazed at eBay to the extent that "How is it that people are earning money without products?" is the question you ask? If so, we are going to introduce you to an Amazon-to-eBay drop shipping, the business model that enables you to sell products on eBay without even holding things. "It is just magic, isn't it?" you say after reading. We, too, think so!

My name is Ravindra, and I have been in eCommerce for so long to know the successes and failures of various ventures. I have observed the difficulties of individuals who are stuck in complicated business models, money spent on goods that could not be sold, and some of them giving in even before they got their first sale. I have seen that dropshipping comes to make life easier and will now turn to money-making business opportunities.

This book is created as your step-by-step guide. Whether you're a professional or a complete novice who wants to master your strategy, I will help you with everything—at the very beginning, helping you to get your store set up and discovering profitable products, automating the listings, and scaling your business.

Compared to traditional business models, drop shipping doesn't require huge initial investments and warehousing or complicated logistics. You simply look for the products you want on Amazon, list them on eBay at a higher price, and when a client purchases, you get the product from Amazon and send it straight to them. Your profit is the gap between your eBay selling price and your Amazon purchase price. Very simple, isn't it? However, just like any other business, the problem is in the details.

CHAPTER 1:
UNDERSTANDING THE AMAZON TO EBAY BUSINESS MODEL (A TO Z)

Welcome to the World of Amazon to eBay Drop shipping!

Anyway, can we make it on the internet without a stock in our hands? Let's discuss it here. By selling Amazon products on eBay, you can easily start an online business without the financial risks associated. Not necessary at first are the warehouse, large upfront investments, or self-owned website. In fact, you will use Amazon and eBay, which are two of the largest online platforms, to form a profitable business.

This chapter will teach you exactly how the drop shipping model functions, why it's so successful, and how you can finally have some financial freedom. The reader will have the opportunity to know each of the steps which will include practical as well as real-world examples to help them on this journey.

How Does Amazon to eBay Dropshipping Work?

Let's pretend that you have the following experience:

1. You find a product on Amazon that everyone wants to own for $50 and you think about it.
2. You promote the identical product on eBay for $70.
3. He directly gets that product on eBay and you charge him $70.
4. You buy the product from Amazon and ship it directly to the eBay buyer's address.
5. You can buy your profit per sale keeping on the round of $10-$15 (eBay fees are not considered).

Well, in this case, that's it! You don't have to store any stock, you don't need to think about the packaging, and you don't need any initial big investment. Your job is to find items that are on a profitable sale, to make a list of them on eBay, and to handle the orders correctly.

Why This Business Model Works So Well

1. **No Inventory, No Risk**

   The traditional way of eCommerce involves a bulk purchase of products and their storage in warehouses. Dropshipping is the only method that eliminates money risk because you only buy the product after you've already made the sale.

2. **Minimal Upfront Investment**

   You don't have to have thousands of dollars to begin. You can have an eBay account, a Payoneer account for receiving payments, and a readiness to learn.

3. **Massive Market Potential**

   Both Amazon and eBay, the market leaders, are visited by millions of potential buyers looking for products every day. You attract these customers without having to spend a lot of money on advertising.

4. **Automation Tools Make Scaling Easy**

   By using the right software, you can easily display hundreds of products, set up the entire order fulfillment system, and monitor price volatility without manual intervention. (We'll cover this in detail in later chapters.)

Step-by-Step Guide to Getting Started

After mastering the essentials, picking the process into a few smaller tasks will become easier.

Step 1: Create an eBay Seller Account

Firstly, if you do not have any eBay account, please follow these actions:

1. Log onto eBay.com and press "Register."

2. Pick "Create a Business Account" from the plans if you want to make profit over a long period.
3. State your information and initiate the rest of the process with the confirmation code you will obtain.
4. Attach your Payoneer account to your eBay Seller Dashboard and then configure it (we will see how to do this in the next section grab).

Step 2: Research Profitable Products

Selecting the most suitable items to be traded is the main aim. Here are some main strategies to find winning products:

1. **Use Zik Analytics** – A great software that tracks eBay, produces a list of the best-selling products and informs you of those that are in vogue.
2. **Check Amazon's Movers & Shakers List** – The part of Amazon where the products that are growing the fastest in real-time are shown.
3. **Look at Competitor Listings** – Try to get to know the top sellers in the field of eBay by analyzing other successful dropshippers' products and then list your products.

🔍 **Pro Tip**: Avoid items with frequent returns, such as electronics, and instead go with the products that are safe to be used every day.

Step 3: List Your First Product on eBay

When you find a good one, the next steps are to list it:

1. Copy the product title and images from Amazon.
2. Enter "Sell" on eBay, and pick a category.
3. Now, insert the title and all SEO tweaks in the first part of this Chapter (5).
4. Decide a more competitive price that allows for a profit margin of yours.

5. Give as much information about a product and its shipping as you can.
6. Publish your product after you are finished and go live!

Step 4: Fulfill Orders & Manage Shipping

When a customer buys your product:

1. Open Amazon and buy the product yourself.
2. In place of your order, indicate the shipping location of the one who buys it.
3. Use the specific Amazon Prime membership to get your delivery quickly, or whenever possible, use only the plain box delivery method.
4. Easily update the tracking ID for eBay so your buyer can know the location of the item.

🚀 **Pro Tip**: If you see an ambiguous "TBA" registration code from Amazon that does not suit eBay specifications, use Bluecare Express to translate it (this will be the topic of Chapter 9).

Step 5: Scale Your Business

After you get a little accustomed to it, you can decide to increase your range of action:

1. Display more items in order to raise the profit of your store.
2. Yaballe can also help you with the process of uploading your items through API integration.
3. Keep an eye on your rivals to adjust your pricing strategy when needed.
4. When you deliver your goods to a ward if they are missing to mention most of the items simply to make suggestions on their list, it is very possible.

Real-Life Success Story: John's Journey to $10K/Month

Here is a school day of mine in the digital world. I am inspired by one of my students, John, about whom I would like to tell you a story. John began with just 10 lists on eBay that he had manually managed. Just right in the first month, he earned about $500 of profit. His self-assurance grew and he used automation software to scale his business. In half a year, he has been earning $10,000 per month in revenue. The secret behind his success was doing consistent work, product search, and hand-me-down automation.

I saw how John did it and hence no one can tell me that you can't do it. You may!

Common Mistakes to Avoid

Before we wrap up this chapter, here are some mistakes beginners often make:

✘ **Overpricing Products**: If the price you are offering is higher than those of your competitors, then the buyers would prefer to buy the cheaper alternatives.

✘ **Ignoring eBay's Policies**: eBay is strictly against the act of cross-fulfillment among retailers such as Amazon. Always obey the best course so that your account is not suspended.

✘ **Failing to Provide Tracking Numbers**: You should always make sure that you update the tracking information to keep your seller rating high.

✘ **Not Scaling the Business**: It's a very common mistake- many people might have a good start, but will stick only to a few products. The more listings, the more chances you have to make sales!

Conclusion: Your Next Steps

Well done! You have successfully acquired knowledge of Amazon-to-eBay dropshipping to such an extent that it feels like you have been to Mars and back. Having finished with the below information, we are headed to the next chapter, in which we will talk about how to incorporate Payoneer to your eBay store so you can receive payments. Do you want to act now? The first step: Sign up for your eBay seller account, decide on a product, and list it today. So, the adventure of setting up your dropshipping business begins from now on! 🚀

Chapter 2: Connecting Your eBay Store to Payoneer

Why You Need Payoneer for eBay Dropshipping

Before you can even start getting money from your eBay success, you need a reliable payment processor. The reason is that PayPal stopped supporting eBay and therefore has become Payoneer the only solution. This is a service that easily lets you go through the deals from eBay to the money being on a card that can be swiped at a local bank ATM without any trouble.

The current approach is to customize your Payoneer account in such a way that it can be linked directly with eBay. In this way, the customer's transactions can be done smoothly in a well-administered currency. Together, we shall deal with the tasks like receiving, withdrawing, and administering money seamlessly.

Step-by-Step Guide: Setting Up Your Payoneer Account

Step 1: Sign Up for Payoneer

1. Access the Payoneer official website.
2. Press "Sign Up & Earn $25" (if it is available, Payoneer usually offers bonuses to new users).
3. Select Individual or Company (If it's your first time, choose Individual).
4. Tell about your personal data:
   - The full name you use in your bank account (you cannot alter it)
   - Email your address
   - Enter your date of birth

5. Continue by filling out your contact details and then click Next.

6. Ask for creating a password and security question.

7. In close quarter, leave bank details for withdrawals (Here you should know that Payoneer is almost available all over the world - it will match most international banks).

8. Submit your application and then just wait for Payoneer to approve it (which is usually done in 24-48 hours).

✏️ **Pro Tip:** Double-check that your name as well as your bank details are accurate in comparison to your official records so that you are not caught up by approval delays.

Step 2: Linking Payoneer to Your eBay Account

After passing the approval of your Payoneer account, you will have to link eBay to it to collect your money.

How to Link Payoneer to eBay

1. Log in to eBay Seller Hub.

2. Click on Payments in the left-hand menu.

3. Opt for Add a payout method and select Payoneer.

4. At this point, Payoneer's login page will open—type in your username and pass and then you should give permission for the connection.

5. Click the link and accept the connection request after which you will be redirected to eBay.

💡 **Tip:** eBay might ask you for some more proving (such as identity confirmation), so have your ID with you in case you have to upload it.

Managing Your Funds: Best Practices

The process to connect Payoneer with eBay should be done from Payoneer's side, where the former will then be able to send money directly to the user's bank account according to the schedule chosen (daily, weekly, or monthly). This is how to properly manage your funds:

1. **Withdraw Funds Smartly:** Do money transfer to the bank's local bank only when the exchange rate is favorable.

2. **Monitor Your Transactions:** You can use the Payoneer dashboard to view payouts, fees, and currency exchange rates.

3. **Use a Business Account:** By expanding the store, e-commerce entrepreneurs should try to get a business Payoneer account which provides better financial management.

🔍 Real-Life Example:

For Sarah, the new seller on the eBay marketplace, receiving cash became the problem due to the discrepancies in the bank's data involved in the payout process. She then, with linking the verified Payoneer site, was able to earn her payments to correct her bank account, which went so smoothly that within 48 hours her payment was completed. She now gets money every week with no difficulties.

Troubleshooting Common Payoneer Issues

While Payoneer offers an impressive solution for payments, yet it is possible for you to come across some problems every once in a while. Below are some of the normal problems and their solutions:

1. **Delayed Payouts:** Look at the eBay payout schedule which must be set to weekly or monthly.

2. **Account Verification Issues:** Make sure that the documents you provide (ID, bank statements) are articulately moist and completely error-free.

3. **Incorrect Bank Details:** You should always check your bank details in the system before withdrawing money from it.

If the issue is still not resolved, then be sure to contact Payoneer Support or get the assistance of eBay customer service.

Conclusion: Get Ready to Start Selling!

After you have successfully set up and linked your Payoneer account, it's time to plunge in and start secure eBay trading. In the following chapter, we shall learn all about Cash Flow & Fund Management—a critical skill in the venture of operating a financially successful dropshipping business.

🔥 **Action Step:** Checking your Payoneer and practicing browsing the dashboard can help you log in now. A clear understanding of your payment flow ahead of the purchase will prevent you from worrying later!

See you in the next chapter! 🚀

Chapter 3:
Cash Flow & Fund Management

The Importance of Managing Your Cash Flow

It is fundamental for any operation to have enough money to carry on. Cash flow is no less than the oils of an engine, and an eBay dropshipping business should be mindful of it too. Having a good grip on your money will let you have no trouble with your dons or workers, paying fees, or even scaling up your business. The following chapter will help you understand the whole process of cash flow management.

Understanding eBay's Payment Process

The cash flow of your business is affected differently by the fixed payout system of eBay compared to the usual cases of almost-instant payment efficiency in traditional businesses.

1. **Buyer Pays eBay**: A customer pays for the item and eBay gets the money first.

2. **eBay Processes the Payment**: eBay takes out some fees and keeps the rest.

3. **Payouts to Payoneer**: eBay, according to your plan (daily, weekly, or monthly), transfers funds to your Payoneer account.

4. **Withdraw to Your Bank**: Once the amount is in Payoneer, it can be shifted to your local bank account.

💡 **Pro Tip**: Make your eBay payouts daily to better plan your cash flow on the one hand and also leave with a balance on the other to make sure the order cost is covered while awaiting funds from the transactions.

Step-by-Step Guide to Managing Cash Flow

Step 1: Keep Track of Your Expenses

Use a spreadsheet or QuickBooks, and set up a simple accounting system for tracking the following:

- **Cost of goods** (Amazon product price)
- **eBay selling fees**
- **Payoneer transaction fees**
- **Additional expenses** (ads, automation tools, etc.)

Step 2: Maintain a Cash Reserve

For example, because eBay currently holds back payments for a while, you should set up a cash reserve for:

- **To keep your business running smoothly** you should lock the new orders and wait for money to receive from the customers.
- **Be ready for more returns and refunds** than you might expect any time.
- **Adding a subscription** to the automation tool.

✓ **Targeted Cash Reserves**: Have a minimum of sales revenue for two weeks kept aside.

Step 3: Increase Your Profit Margins

For sustainable profits, apply this formula:

Profit = Selling Price (eBay) − Amazon Cost − eBay Fees − Payoneer Fees

🔍 **Example:**

- **Cost of product on Amazon** = $30
- **Selling price for eBay listing** = $50
- **Final value fee on eBay (14%)**: $7
- **$1 is charged for using Payoneer services**
- **Profit**: $12 each sale

💡 **Tip**: Estimate your precise profits by using an eBay Fee Calculator or similar cost calculating tools.

Common Cash Flow Mistakes to Avoid

✖ Not everyone can afford to pay a little bit of their earnings from eBay and other places for a fee. Use a cash reserve to fund the orders and take control of your situation when you want to make a margin, as the platforms charge some money. Sometimes you may find yourself selling a product for nothing more than the fee.

Automating Fund Management for Efficiency

If managing finances manually seems overwhelming, consider automation tools:

- **Yaballe**: Receipts and invoices are automatically generated by Yaballe eBay sales cost and deductions. It is also an all-in-one eBay dropshipping automation tool.

- **AutoDS**: Create and fulfill orders easily on eBay and see net profits, eBay, and shipping costs on a single page. Join 1,500 eBay sellers that use AutoDS to create and fulfill orders automatically.

- **QuickBooks or Wave**: The online invoicing app that ties the service together with ease is E-Invoice Factoring Service. Use QuickBooks for tax preparation or combine it with payroll software to make it even more convenient.

Real-Life Example:

Acheng, one of our popular dropshipping customers, expanded his business after just one month! eBay has a vested interest in his business for a long time. Mike, a dropshipper, scaled his store quickly but ran into cash flow problems because he didn't account for eBay's payout delays. By switching to daily payouts and keeping a cash reserve, he stabilized his business and tripled his revenue in three months.

Conclusion: Keep Your Finances in Check

Thus, money management is the basic thing when you are doing your business as an eBay dropshipper profitably. In terms of improving the working capital situation, you have three options, which are tracking your expenses, having a cash buffer, and developing masterful skills to maximize your income.

🔥 **Action Step**: Analyze your current cash flow planning, edit the payment schedule of eBay, and create a simple expense tracking method.

CHAPTER 4:
AUTOMATION SOFTWARE SETUP & CONFIGURATION

Why Automation is Essential for Dropshipping Success

When your dropshipping business starts to grow, you can end up getting overloaded by creating listings manually, carrying out orders, and even controlling inventory. **Automation**, that's where it comes in. By using the right tools, you can increase your performance and reduce time to focus on strategy and expansion. **BY THE RIGHT BOTS YOU WILL be amazed.**

This section will give you a step-by-step guide through the automated software's setup. There will also be guides on the configuration and what is the best way to use it to your advantage.

Choosing the Right Automation Software

As regards dropshipping, there are numerous tools in the market, but these are the most recommended for Amazon to eBay dropshipping:

- **Yaballe** – Most recommended, it is helpful for bulk listing and all that inventory management in real-time.

- **AutoDS** – The best choice for a person looking for a software program to monitor stock and price changes in one place.

- **DS Titan** – The most preferred product research and filling orders in just one click is the main USP of DS Titan.

- **Zik Analytics** – Aids in selecting that niche that is profitable and in analyzing the degree of competition in that field.

✅ **Pro Tip**: If you are just a newbie, consider this option for your initial phase: go for **Yaballe** and **AutoDS**, mainly to do the repetitive work in an automatic manner.

Step-by-Step Guide: Setting Up Yaballe

Step 1: Register & Connect Your eBay Store

- **Yaballe's website** is the place to go if you'd like to avail an account on them.

- Just choose the **eBay plan** that suits your business very well.

- **eBay authorization** must be done in such a way that it should be the last step of integrating the e-commerce product.

- Then, the text should appear as a link to the **table of contents (Dashboard)** from where the user will be able to get the settings that he will need.

Step 2: Configure Basic Settings

- Now go to **Settings**. Then click **General** to get to the settings list.

- Start with a recommended value of the default one, which is **15-20%**, and continue.

- Enable **Auto-Tracking Update**, which is designed to make sure that your package tracking numbers are in sync with your eBay account.

Step 3: Bulk Product Listing

- Collect **ASINs** from Amazon by using **ASINGrabber** Chrome extension.

- Insert these ASINs into Yaballe's **Bulk Lister** and submit.

- Analyze the **product titles** for more SEO optimization (refer to Chapter 5 for optimization tips).

- Hit the **List Items** button on the page, and the products will be submitted to the eBay shop for sale.

🔍 **Example**: A dropshipper, Lisa, used Yaballe to list 500+ products in one click. She managed to sell an extra 30% of the goods while only automating the listing process within a week.

Setting Up AutoDS for Seamless Order Fulfillment

Step 1: Connect Your eBay Account

- First and foremost, you need to **register an account** for AutoDS.

- Now go to the **"Add Store"** tab and connect your seller account to eBay.

Step 2: Enable Automated Order Fulfillment

- Click on **Orders > Automation Settings**.

- In order to save yourself some time, put the **Auto Order Processing** on to handle the automatic processing of orders.

- Turn on **Price & Stock Monitoring** so as to see the changes on Amazon.

Step 3: Set Up Auto-Repricing

- First of all, go to the **Pricing Rules** area.

- Enter your **minimum and maximum margins** of profit.

- Allow **auto-adjustment** of price depending on the prices of competitors.

✅ **Pro Tip**: Besides, the program allows a message to be sent automatically to buyers, thus improving **Customer Service** and minimizing refunds.

Managing Inventory with Automation Tools

Once you set up the automation tools, you can:

- **Check stock counts** – The supplies are kept in stock to avoid the loss of products through cancellation.

- **Attach tracking numbers** – Buyers are auto-informed to track the shipment process.

- **Eliminate mismatched prices** – When Amazon updates costs accordingly, dynamic price adaptation is a must.

📌 **Case Study**: John, an eBay seller, employed AutoDS for the first time. These three months, he managed to solve his stock shortage, which caused a 70% reduction in the client's refusal to cancel an order. He also managed to achieve a turnover of **$15,000 per month**.

Avoiding Common Automation Mistakes

❌ **Too Rapidly Overloading Your Store** – While slow increases in listings can help you avoid eBay limits.
❌ **Price Fluctuations Are Not Taken into Account** – Ensure you have a system of automatic price observation working all the time.

✘ **Inadequately Writing Product Titles** – The titles do not convey the right message, and therefore, the products get fewer views.

Conclusion: Scale Smart with Automation

Use the duo of **Yaballe** and **AutoDS** to simplify the entire product listing, order processing, and inventory management tasks, thanks to which you will be able to develop your business further.

🔥 **Action Step**: Set one automation tool this day and arrange it based on the steps given above, further driving your revenues.

In the next chapter, we will cover **'Increasing Your eBay Store Limits for Higher Profits'**—which is a major step that enables the dropshipping business to grow. Keep an eye on us! 🚀

Chapter 5: Increasing Your eBay Store Limits for Higher Profits

Why Increasing Your eBay Store Limits Matters

Restrictions for how many items you can list and commission per month exist when you originally start to sell on eBay. Rules like these were created to protect people from fraud and to allow those who are newly joining to grow a satisfied relationship with their clients. But it is important to expand these restrictions if your objective is to grow your business with dropshipping.

This chapter tells you in detail how to proceed with the request and approval of higher eBay limits on selling. Also, I will guide you through different tactics successful sellers have used to be approved quickly.

Understanding eBay Selling Limits

eBay sets limits based on your account's history and performance. The main types of limits are:

- **Account Limits** – Make it easy for someone to sell on eBay with lower entry barriers like listing fees and limits (e.g., 10 items and $500 in sales per month for new sellers) – This is for the normal users and people who are only just starting to sell on eBay. It is not fair for them with the current system, does not meet the customer's expectations, and is the main reason for abandoning eBay.

- **Category Limits** – Prevent that from happening by letting buyers know about the upcoming sales a few days in advance. It is wise for the sellers to be flexible and considerate with their prospective buyers with the goal of maintaining a good reputation despite any setbacks in meeting the demands and needs of the buyers.

- **Item-specific limits** – Are pre-released products like games, software, and physical movies or movies that are one-of-a-kind releases. For these highest-risk items, eBay has put in place some serious restrictions on them.

💡 **Pro Tip**: Your eBay seller dashboard shows your current limits. Go to **My eBay > Selling > Monthly Limits** to see them.

Step-by-Step Guide: How to Increase Your Selling Limits

Step 1: Build a Strong Seller Reputation

In advance of hunting down bigger boundaries, make sure your account's state is such that it is at the top of the game:

- Maintain a **100% positive feedback score**.
- Ship orders on time and upload tracking numbers.
- Respond promptly to customer inquiries.
- Avoid order cancellations and disputes.

🔍 **Example**: Jake, a new dropshipper, always had his defective rate within **0.5%** and still got a five-star rating for three months. He decided to ask for an increase in limits, and eBay said yes only after **24 hours**.

Step 2: Request a Selling Limit Increase

After building a strong record, through the following steps, one can ask for a raise:

- Navigate to your **eBay Seller Hub**.

- Go to **My eBay > Selling** and search for the section that indicates your selling limits.

- Click on **"Request a Limit Increase"**.

- eBay will go through the analysis of your account activity and it can even give you the automatic limit increase.

- If no automatic increase is provided, then you should contact eBay support.

- Call the **seller support** of eBay or use the live chat option.

- Tell the company why you need more limits (e.g., higher demand, stable record, and verified supplier connections).

✅ **Tip**: Be friendly and talk to eBay's representatives respectfully. Emphasize your remarkable performance metrics and the fact that you are determined towards excellent customer service.

Step 3: Provide Proof of Reliable Suppliers

If eBay asks for additional verification, be prepared to show:

- **Invoices or receipts** from reputable suppliers (e.g., Amazon, Walmart).

- The documents of a **business** you have registered (if applicable).

- **Payoneer or bank statements** which are used to show that you have the money and are credible.

Case Morde: Laura, purchasing from Amazon, had to show her eBay invoices to double her limits in under a week. She said the response was fast.

Alternative Methods to Increase Limits

Turn these others over if yours doesn't work out.

1. **Open a Second eBay Account**

- With eBay's multiple account users policy, users can open a second account and join it to a separate Payoneer account for split sales.

- Using the old account, you may do the same thing that would make a steady increase on this account. Then go on.

2. **Use Business Registration to Enhance Your Profile**

- Turn your eBay account into a **business account (My eBay > Account Settings > Upgrade to Business)**.

- It is not uncommon for business accounts to automatically be allowed to sell high.

3. **Scale with eBay Promoted Listings**

- Speeding up with **eBay Promoted Listings**, the volume of your sales is going to help you to get quicker to your profit possibilities.

- Spending **5-10%** of your ad budget will lift your sales by an order of magnitude.

Top Mistakes to Avoid

✗ **Wanting a higher credit limit too early** – You need to have at least **1 month** of completed sales with a minimum of **30 transactions** before you can request maximum selling limits.

✗ **Failing to meet the standards of eBay's return policy** – In case you have a lot of shipping issues, such as high return rates, and you tend to send packages out late, you are decreasing your chances.

✗ **Not being able to provide evidence on where you got the goods** – Once eBay asks for proof, get your supplier invoices ready.

Ending: Scale Your Business Properly

The upping of your eBay selling limits is a major move to grow your dropshipping business. In a constant manner, by applying good store performance through the correct strategy and the use of innovative approaches, one can achieve the store's higher revenue potential all the time.

🔥 **Action Step**: Log in to **eBay Seller Hub** and look at your existing sales restrictions. If you are qualified, please request an increase and start creating new listings for your products.

In the next chapter, **Shipping, Returns, and Payment Policies Setup** will be taken—we will ensure your store is running well with clear policies in place. So keep an eye on it! 🚀

Chapter 6:
Shipping, Returns, and Payment Policies Setup

Why Clear Store Policies Matter

The configuration of shipping, refunds, and payment plans should be properly done so that the buying process goes smoothly. These regulations offer sales, improve customer satisfaction, and eBay rankings.

Setting Up Shipping Policies

Step 1: Choosing the Right Shipping Options

eBay provides various shipping opportunities. Nevertheless, you as a dropshipper who is using Amazon or Walmart should focus on these:

1. **Standard Shipping (3-5 business days)** – Suitable for Amazon Prime orders.
2. **Expedited Shipping (1-3 business days)** – Very good for products in high demand.
3. **Economy Shipping (5-10 business days)** – Suitable for not urgent items.

🔍 **Example:** If you get a product from Amazon with Prime, set Shipping Standard to 3-5 business days.

Step 2: Creating a Shipping Policy

1. Go to eBay Business Policies (Click Here).
2. Click Create Policy > Shipping Policy.
3. Set handling time to 1-2 business days.
4. Choose free shipment to increase your sales rates.
5. Click Save and apply to all listings.

💡 **Tip:** Free shipping leads to more sales and growth among peers.

Configuring Return Policies

Step 1: Selecting the Best Return Option

1. **30-Day Free Returns (Recommended)** – Grows buyer trust and security.

2. **30-Day Buyer Pays Return Shipping** – May apply to certain categories of items with high risk.

3. **No Returns Accepted** – Should not be done, as it can be a block for buyers.

📌 **Example:** A seller has an eBay return policy of 30-Day Free Returns, and in consequence, he noticed an increase in sales of 15% within a month.

Step 2: Making a Refund Policy

1. Go to eBay Business Policies.

2. Click Create Policy > Return Policy.

3. Now, make a selection of the first option, which is 30-day Free Returns.

4. Click Save and apply to all listings.

🚀 **Tip:** The issue might be raised with the help of free returns, and you will even notice an uptick in search results.

Setting Up Payment Policies

Step 1: Enabling eBay Managed Payments

Starting this year, eBay automatically distributes the funds either to Payoneer or into your own bank account.

1. Go to eBay Seller Hub (Click Here).
2. Click Payments > Payout Settings.
3. Be sure your Payoneer account is linked.
4. Pick the payout schedule of your preference (Daily, Weekly, Monthly).

🔍 **Example:** Payouts that are carried out once a week enable the cash flow of a company to remain steady.

Step 2: Creation of Payment Policy

1. Visit the Business Policies option.
2. Hit Create Policy > Payment Policy.
3. Turn Immediate Payment On to avoid orders becoming unpaid.
4. Click Save and apply it to every listing.

✓ **Tip:** Immediate payment forbids unnecessary order cancellations.

Handling Returns and Refunds Efficiently

Step 1: Processing Returns on eBay

1. Go to eBay Seller Hub > Apply for Refund.

2. Greenlight return requests that meet your rules.

3. Fill in a prepaid shipping label (if you provide free returns).

4. Proceed with a refund when the item is received.

Step 2: Managing Refunds via Amazon

1. Sign in to Amazon Orders.

2. Select Return or Replace Items.

3. Pick Refund to Gift Balance in order to reuse the resources.

4. If required, load the return label from eBay to Amazon.

🔍 **Example:** A seller who used the Amazon return system successfully decreased the losses due to returns.

Avoiding Common Policy Mistakes

✘ **Not Offering Free Returns** – The store is less visible and less trusted.

✘ **Setting Long Handling Times** – eBay tends to favor sellers who give the orders one of a handling time.

✘ **Failing to Enable Immediate Payment** – This makes for unpaid orders.

Conclusion: Optimize Policies for Success

Configured policies well are great customer satisfiers, savings, and higher conversions.

🔥 **Action Step:** Get up to date with eBay Business Policies today and keep all transactions going smoothly.

Now on: Product Listing Techniques—how to generate top-rated, conversion-aided listings. 🚀

Chapter 7:
Product Listing Strategies

Why Optimized Listings Matter

An eBay listing that is well optimized ups the promotion, grabs shoppers, and spins the sales wheel. Listings without proper structure, on the other hand, may be filtered out from the search results, thus reducing the possibility of making a sale. In this chapter, I'll show you the detailed procedure of creating captivating listings that will rank better and will convert more people.

Step 1: Choosing the Right Products

Not all products are good to be sold on eBay. Put emphasis on the following ones:

1. **High-demand, low-competition items** – Use Zik Analytics or eBay's trending section

2. **Products with consistent sales history** – Check eBay's Sold Listings

3. **Reliable suppliers** – Source from Amazon, Walmart, or wholesale platforms

🔍 **Example:** A seller has researched eBay trends and introduced products in the pet accessories niche, they have increased their profits by 40% within only 3 months.

Step 2: Writing an Optimized Title

Your title should be keyword-rich and clear. Follow these guidelines:

1. ✅ **Include main keywords** (e.g., "Wireless Bluetooth Headphones Noise Cancelling")

2. ✅ **Spare self redundant words** (e.g., "Best Quality Brand New!")

3. ✓ **Use all 80 spaces for letters and punctuation**

📌 **Tip:** Discover the hottest keywords within Terapeak Product Research tool (in eBay Seller Hub) to further bulk up conversion rates, and hence, profits!

Step 3: Crafting a Winning Description

Your product description should be brief, descriptive, and interesting:

1. **Begin with the use of the main features** (e.g., "The sound is so clear, the battery can last for 12 hours.")

2. **Give the main ideas in a few sentences and a bullet list.**

3. **Bringing into focus the refund policy and delivering details at the shipping stage is a way of ensuring the customer gets to enjoy the many benefits offered.**

📌 **Example:** A seller was able to boost their conversion rate by 25% upon converting their design from being a paragraph to bullet points, and giving clear benefits.

Step 4: Using High-Quality Images

Pictures that appear excellent and are without flaws can be of great help:

1. **Clinch front, back, close-up, and packaging shots with at least 5 pictures.**

2. **Screen resolution of at least 1000x1000 pixels should be the minimum.**

3. **Watermarks or logos inclusive of third parties violating eBay's policies are two examples of what to stay away from.**

🔍 **Tip:** Employ the free tools such as Canva to improve images before uploading.

Step 5: Setting Competitive Pricing

Pricing makes the item more visible and increases sales:

1. **Check out the prices set by your opponents and make sure that your deals are reasonably priced to lure customers.**
2. **Try eBay's Price Match Strategy** – Lowering prices can improve rankings.
3. **Tools like Best Offer and Volume Discounts were employed to invite customers to buy.**

🚀 **Example:** A seller impressed 30% with the sales-increasing prices and packaging them up, gaining the customer loyalty.

Step 6: Enabling Promoted Listings

Get noticed by placing out eBay Promoted Listings:

1. **Go to Seller Hub > Advertising Dashboard.**
2. **Choose the products and apply a promotion (2-5% is OK).**
3. **Check your results and improve your ads if necessary.**

✅ **Tip:** Focus on high-profits potential items to pad your wallet.

Conclusion: Create Listings That Sell

Optimizing a product listing is the key to being noticeable and therefore to increase sales. By identifying products, which are ultimate, by using tempting headliners, by writing clear and genuine descriptions, and including promotions, you can indeed elevate your eBay business a lot.

🔥 **Action Step:** Apply the techniques presented, while improving your ads and keep an eye on how they do during the next 6 days.

Next up: eBay Keyword Research—where to get the most appropriate keywords to get a top-ranking in the search results. 🚀

CHAPTER 8:
eBay Keyword Research

Why Keyword Research Matters

Key phrases through which your items stand out from among others in eBay search outcomes. Advising the most suitable ones raises the attention-grabbing of your product, invites buyers, and results in sales increasing.

Step 1: Finding High-Performing Keywords

1. **Use eBay's Search Bar** – Beginning to type a product name can display auto-fill options.

2. **Examine Competitor Listings** – Study the keywords used by the top sellers first.

3. **Look for Terapeak Product Research** – Come across the hot products with best sales supported by the related keywords.

4. **Google Keyword Planner** – It can make use of sites to come up with relevant terms that are usually searched for.

🔍 **Example**: A merchant took a sales increase by 20% by simply gaining steps ahead using Terapeak sales key phrases.

Step 2: Optimizing Your Listings

✅ Use keywords such as "Wireless Bluetooth Earbuds Noise Cancelling" that are popular in the title

✅ Have several versions of the same keyword phrase (like "Bluetooth Earphones" and "Wireless Headphones")

✓ Allow keywords to flow through naturally in the profiles

🚀 **Tip**: Instead of keyword stuffing, use relevant terms in a natural flow.

Step 3: Monitoring and Adjusting

1. **One short-term forecast setting** is to watch performance quickly in Seller Hub.

2. **Produce algorithms** that boost your search ranking through a content update.

3. **Design many combinations** and follow changes in outcomes.

✈ **Example**: A seller optimized their product titles monthly, which helped to boost the traffic by 15%.

Conclusion: Rank Higher with Smart Keywords

Optimizing your descriptions and making sure it is the right buyers that are finding your listings is the outcome of effective keyword research. Keywords must be properly tailored to be ahead.

🔥 **Action Step**: Research whether your listings are popular because of the keywords or if it's the latest zeitgeist and then use them as a basis for your keyword planning.

Next up: Writing awesome Titles for Higher Click-Through Rates. 🚀

Chapter 9:
Title Optimization for Higher Click-Through Rates

Why Title Optimization Matters

Your eBay title will be the first thing a buyer will see. A good topic title will not only be appealing to buyers but also will lead to more traffic and finally result in an increased sale.

Step 1: Writing an Effective Title

1. ✓ **Use all 80 characters** – Remember to add multiple keywords and synonyms into your title.

2. ✓ **Include primary keywords first** – Begin the title by using the main keywords.

3. ✓ **Avoid unnecessary words** – The words "Best" and "Wow!" can be omitted.

4. ✓ **Use variations** – In addition to the original keyword, add elements that will attract buyers' interest.

🔍 **Example**: Instead of "Bluetooth Headphones," try "Wireless Bluetooth Headphones Noise Cancelling Over-Ear".

Step 2: Tools for Better Titles

1. **eBay's Search Bar** – eBay's search tool can be beneficial in finding popular keywords.

2. **Terapeak Product Research** – To build good titles find out the best way to write your title with the best product research as the description and follow these tips.

3. **Competitor Analysis** – Compose titles that are stronger than the titles of your main competitors.

🖋 **Tip**: Use one of the following ways whenever you are about to update your titles: Look at the buyers' needs and then create your titles accordingly. Regularly update your titles to match buyer trends.

Step 3: Monitoring and Adjusting

1. **Monitor your seller hub click-through rates at eBay to track your performance**
2. **Modify the titles and compare click-through rate to observe the results**
3. **Refine from eBay search trends for the best marketing and inclusion of keywords on titles to make your product easily found**

📌 **Example**: A seller found out that if he changed the product title every two weeks, he had an 18% rise in sales.

Conclusion: Improve Titles, Boost Sales

A well-optimized title is the key to your listing's success. It never hurts to push the envelope; build in contingency plans for all the inevitable changes.

🔥 **Action Step**: Make at least five product titles today your priority to show up in the search results as often as possible.

Chapter 10: Automating Buyer Messages to Improve Customer Experience

Why Automate Buyer Messages?

Assuring quick and consistent communication with buyers enlarges their satisfaction and certainly is the cause of positive feedback. Automated messages allow wasting no time while still enabling your customers to get a professional and helpful service from you.

Step 1: Setting Up Automated Messages

1. ✅ **Welcome Message** – Immediate sending to thank the buyer for the purchase.

2. ✅ **Order Confirmation** – Assuring the buyer that his/her order is being processed.

3. ✅ **Shipping Notification** – Offering tracking details when the item ships.

4. ✅ **Follow-Up Request for Feedback** – The buyers are encouraged to share good experiences.

🚀 **Tip:** Be sure you give a warm, friendly, and professional message to the receiver to increase the feeling of security.

Step 2: Using eBay's Automation Tools

1. **eBay's Selling Manager Pro** – Orders are automatically updated.

2. **Third-Party Tools (e.g., AutoDS, Yaballe)** – Supports advanced automation.

3. **Saved Message Templates** – These are already typed responses for frequently asked questions.

🔍 **Example:** A seller automates his thank-you messages and as a result, he got a 25% increase in positive feedback.

Step 3: Monitoring and Adjusting

1. **Examine how many buyers have responded** – Are your customers actively responding to your messages?

2. **Time the messaging** – Create and send follow-up messages a few days after item delivery.

3. **Choose the most suitable words in the message** – This will make your point clear and will present you as a professional.

📌 **Example:** Changing time for a follow-up message resulted in a 15% increase in purchasing frequency.

Conclusion: Enhance Customer Satisfaction Effortlessly

Optimization of the buyer's automatic message system guarantees that the interaction with the customer becomes more efficient and a stronger relationship is built. On the other hand, proper timing and detailed information provided will bring trust to the customer's side, thus, they will come back again in the future.

🔥 **Action Step:** Implement at least one automated buyer message as soon as possible.

CHAPTER 11: SCANNING AMAZON DROPSHIPPERS GOODS IN BULK AND DROPPING THEIR LEADING ITEMS

Why Competitor Dropshipper Identification Matters

One of the most efficient methods to discover which products would be the most lucrative ones is by studying Amazon-to-eBay super dropshippers. You can save a lot of time and increase your sales quickly by identifying the best-selling products and selling them, instead of testing different products to see which ones will do best.

Step 1: Spotting Amazon Dropshippers in Bulk

1. ✅ **Use eBay's Search Filters** – Search for products dropshipped from Amazon.

2. ✅ **Look for Matching Product Titles and Images** – A lot of dropshippers use the exact product names and images of Amazon.

3. ✅ **View Seller Profiles** – See if a seller has a large number of similar products for sale and if he/she ships them quickly.

🔍 **For instance**: A seller identified 50+ dropshippers after looking for "Ships from Amazon" in eBay listings.

Step 2: Using Tools to Scan Competitor Stores

1. **Zik Analytics** – (NYSE:EBAY) reviews are the best on that platform and it even discloses $1.5 billion in annual sales, $2.6 billion in cash, and cash equivalents, and $654 million in operating activities. Its $900-million free-cash-flow mechanical model helps investors capitalize on this high ROE. ZIK

Analytics informs eBay sellers and shows their best-performing items.

2. **AutoDS Finder** – It helps you find the most sought-after dropshipping products online. AutoDS is among the best brands.

3. **Yaballe's Seller Scanner** – It helps you to find out the most profitable and popular products of your competitors. The app is one of the best to be used for those sellers who want to be more efficient in doing their work and improve their sales as a result.

✒ **Tip**: Focusing only on the sellers who have been with the platform for the longest time and had the highest percentage of excellent feedback, as well as multiple relatively recent sales per product, can be beneficial.

Step 3: Sniping Their Best-Sellers

1. **Find High-Selling Items** – From the commonly purchased first options of the eBay brand, Zik Analytics helps to segregate out the top-selling products by up to 40%.

2. **List Similar Products** – You will be sourcing the top-selling items of a competitor such as Amazon thus the same or better quality.

Step 4: Scaling Up with Bulk Listing Tools

1. **Yaballe Bulk Lister** – You can easily list multiple items from Amazon to eBay in record time.

2. **AutoDS Bulk Upload** – This feature will automatically upload and update your products.

3. **DS Titan** – It erases all the hassles of inventory and pricing; handling everything efficiently.

🔍 **Tip**: When you are testing, choose the product category that gave the best performance.

Conclusion: Reverse-Engineer Success

When you spy on Amazon dropshippers, you will save time compared to other sellers in terms of research and product selection. Stealing their top-sellers and massively improving your listings will help you to scale your business even faster and make more money along the way.

🔥 **Action Step**: E.g., Use Zik Analytics or AutoDS today to search for at least five of your main competitors (or as many as you can) and include the top-selling items they have listed.

Next up: Coping we just proceeded with: Bulk Sale on Amazon Guise, and Luring It into Wallmart with Zoro's Help. 🚀

CHAPTER 12:
COPYING AMAZON PRODUCTS IN BULK AND LISTING THEM ON eBAY IN THREE CLICKS

Why Bulk Listing is a Game-Changer

Listing products one by one manually can sometimes be time-consuming. You can quickly import multiple Amazon products to your eBay store by using bulk listing tools and save hours of work while, at the same time, maximizing profits with just a few clicks.

Step 1: Choosing the Right Bulk Listing Tool

By one of the following tools, you can make the import of the products automatic:

1. **Yaballe Bulk Lister** – Helps you to easily copy Amazon listings to eBay.

2. **AutoDS Bulk Uploader** – Auto-syncs product details and pricing.

3. **DS Titan** – Makes bulk uploads and stock updates quickly and accurately doable.

🚀 **Tip:** Pick a solution that would support this both (eBay integration and stock and price automatic updates) and would be easy to use for your customers.

Step 2: Importing Amazon Products in Three Clicks

1. **Copy the Product Links** – Instead of doing this manually, I suggest you use a bulk ASIN extractor like ASINGrabber.

2. **Paste the ASIN into the Bulk Lister** – Upon getting the ASINs, open your chosen tool of Yaballe, AutoDS or DS Titan

and then paste the ASINs that you have copied from the previous step.

3. **Choose 'List Items'** – With just one click, the program will take care of the rest, it will fully complete listings and set details on eBay.

🔍 **Example:** One seller uploaded more than 100 items through Yaballe in less than 10 minutes and skyrocketed sales by 50% in one month.

Step 3: Optimizing Listings After Bulk Upload

After the bulk import, modify your listings to become the bright spot of the search result list:

✓ **Edit Titles for SEO** – Try to find the most viewed keywords and add them into the header of your titles to increase their visibility.

✓ **Adjust Pricing** – To be sure you are making money, put the prices at the level that will ensure you are ahead of the competition.

✓ **Check Descriptions & Images** – Don't just resort to manufacturer descriptions that might prove not to be eBay-specific.

🚀 **Tip:** Leverage eBay's Product Research Terapeak to dig deep and find the most competent keywords that fit your titles.

Step 4: Automating Price & Stock Updates

Because of the rapid changes in Amazon rates and stock, the tools that allow us to automate are extremely important:

1. **Enable Auto Price Updates** – Tools like AutoDS adapt prices according to the last Amazon pricing.

2. **Sync Stock Availability** – You can control stock very effectively, only sell what is in stock, and avoid refunds with the real-time stock updates enabled.

3. **Set Break-Even Margins** – Price your products so that you will still make a profit after paying eBay fees and buying the product from the wholesaler.

An illustration for you: AutoDS even helped a user who sells things on the internet to meet the price of the items with the customer's willingness to buy and thereafter, the user was able to grow his profit by 20%.

Conclusion: Scale Faster with Bulk Listing

Use the listers that are designed for a dropshipping business, and you will succeed in building a business that is efficient in scaling. By automating product imports, optimizing listings, and setting up stock updates you can save time while increasing sales.

🔥 **Action Step:** Entrepreneurs should stick to a single platform and enjoy its benefits, which include automating tasks, importation of goods, and solving stock issues.

Next up: (Bonus) **Secret Method to Find Walmart Dropshippers in Bulk.** 🚀

Chapter 13:
(Bonus) Secret Method to Find Walmart Dropshippers in Bulk

Why Finding Walmart Dropshippers Matters

While many eBay-to-Amazon dropshippers, the truth is however that Walmart is a goldmine that is yet to be touched. Walmart has fewer competition and in most cases, the prices they offer are also lower which makes the profit margin higher. To identify Walmart dropshippers in bulk will give you a strategic advantage.

Step 1: Identifying Walmart Dropshippers on eBay

1. ✅ **Search for Common Walmart Product Titles**

    A majority of dropshippers simply reiterate a certain Walmart product title.

2. ✅ **Look for Stock Photos**

    The sellers using Walmart images are definitely the dropshippers.

3. ✅ **Check Fast Shipping Times**

    Most Walmart+ products are delivered for free within two days, which is very similar to Amazon Prime.

🔍 **Example:** A seller discovered over 30 Walmart dropshippers by searching "Mainstays 4-Cube Organizer," a Walmart-exclusive brand.

Step 2: Using Tools to Scan Competitor Stores

1. **Zik Analytics**

   Points out the top selling Walmart-to-eBay dropshippers (according to their sales).

2. **AutoDS Scanner**

   Picks up bulk figures from sellers trying to compete with similar items.

3. **Ecomhunt**

   Supplies some information that helps to track some products so that you know what is in trend at Wal-Mart.

🚀 **Tip:** Pay attention to the sellers that have a hundred percent satisfactory feedback score and a lot of recent sales.

Step 3: Sniping Their Best-Selling Products

1. **Find High-Selling Items**

   Come and run the Zik Analytics software to discover the list of best-selling items of your competitor.

2. **List the Same or Better Products**

   Either the same items or, if possible, the currently upgraded ones should be sourced from Walmart.

3. **Optimize Your Listing**

   Come up with a good title and write an impressive description to secure better visibility on the search engine results pages.

4. **Price Competitively**

   Give a little to no discount or a better option as far as delivery is concerned.

📌 **Example:** One seller imitated what had been a best-selling product of Walmart and got a 35% increase in the income of the store within two months.

Step 4: Scaling Your Walmart to eBay Dropshipping Business

1. **Be sure to use the Bulk Listing Tools**

   AutoDS, Yaballe, and DS Titan in order to save some time.

2. **Keep an Eye on the Price & Stock Changes**

   Walmart frequently adjusts the quantity of items available on its inventory.

3. **Explore Movement to the Development of Your Private Brand (OEM)**

   Go into the organic brands like Mainstays and Better Homes & Gardens, that are available globally in Walmart stores.

🔍 **Tip:** Do not take the risk of selling restricted brands. Otherwise, you might be banned from eBay by violating policies.

Conclusion: Leverage Walmart for Higher Profits

The discovery of Walmart dropshippers and the analysis of their performance are competent actions that grant you a significant competitive edge. Establish a procedure that enables you to identify their most popular items and make improvements to them, so that you can achieve growth rapidly and make more profits.

● Action Step:

Download Zik Analytics or AutoDS on your devices and later identify a minimum of five Walmart dropshippers. As a follow-through, pick their five most popular items and add them to your list.

More to come: Efficiently Upgrading Track Numbers for Orders. 🚀

Chapter 14:
Updating Tracking Numbers for Orders Efficiently

Why Updating Tracking Numbers is Essential

To quote track of what is happening, timely updates offer customers the satisfaction they want, and eBay maintains the standards sellers commit to. If the tracking number is inaccurate or not up-to-date, buyers can use this in dispute, leave negative feedback, and give low seller ratings to the seller.

Step 1: Understanding eBay's Tracking Policies

1. **Insert the tracking number of the product with the specified handling time** – eBay does not accept tracking that is outside the handling time specified by the seller.

2. **Picking the right carrier** – The postal carrier should be eligible to use eBay (e.g., USPS, UPS, FedEx).

3. **Keep an eye on the tracking of the shipping** – Proactively resolve any issues that come up if the shipment is late.

🔍 **Example:** A seller who consistently updated their tracking information on eBay saw a 15% rise in positive feedback.

Step 2: Automating Tracking Updates

1. **AutoDS Tracking System** – Can automatically import the tracking data from your suppliers.

2. **Yaballe Auto-Tracking** – After conversion of the TBA numbers and packing operations, sellers have a tracking number.

3. **BlueCare Express (BCE)** – Is mostly a platform to scale cryptocurrency and a warehouse to sell and distribute vending machines, where Mr. Larry Meneus is also a Co-founder & CEO simultaneously, is an International Arbitrage Group member.

🚀 **Tip:** Enable automated tracking updates so as not to lose money or time on mistakes.

Step 3: Manually Updating Tracking Numbers

If automation is not possible, the tracking will be updated manually.

1. **Retrieve Tracking from Supplier** – Don't forget to enter your supplier's data directly into the eBay seller interface or ask him for a consignment on eBay.

2. **Go to eBay Seller Hub** – In eBay Seller Hub, go to the orders section, and then select the 'Awaiting Shipment' subsection.

3. **Enter Tracking Details** – Respond with a thumbs up or down to a new question on eBay by typing the word "yes" and the word "no" into the system and resume by inserting the tracking number.

4. **Select the Carrier** – Make sure to choose the suggested shipping carrier from the drop-down list.

5. **Click Confirm & Save** – Verify that the change is reflected in your order history and simply update it.

🚀 **Example:** A seller enlarged his revenue by 30% by manually updating tracking info for each and every sale.

Step 4: Handling Amazon Logistics (AMZL) Tracking Numbers

Amazon may use TBA as a tracking number, and it may not be known by eBay. The option to change them is to:

1. **BlueCare Express (BCE)** – The system gives you real tracking numbers depending on the type you choose.

2. **Third-Party Trackers** – Places such as TrackMyPackage can give you other ways to detect such numbers.

🔍 **Tip:** Make sure all of your tracking numbers are eBay-friendly so that no complaints occur between you and eBay customers.

Conclusion: Stay Ahead with Timely Tracking Updates

Having up-to-date information on tracking numbers ensures a seller of a healthy seller rating and it gives the buyer a smooth trust experience. The way you should work with your tracking updates depends on whether you use software automation or manual entry.

🔥 **Action Step:** Install a self-propelled code that updates your tracking automatically or make a pact to update it manually every day.

Next: Making eBay-Compatible the Amazon Logistics Tracking Numbers.

Chapter 15: Converting AMZL Tracking Numbers to eBay-Compatible Formats

Why Converting AMZL Tracking Matters

Amazon Logistics (AMZL) tracking numbers are not acknowledged by eBay, hence tracking details sent by suppliers that eBay uses may list fewer tracking events than they actually have. Converting AMZL tracking to an eBay-accepted format ensures smooth order processing and reduces disputes.

Step 1: Understanding the AMZL Tracking Issue

1. ✓ The TBA code that is provided by Amazon is an invalid code valid on eBay – eBay does not support AMZL tracking.

2. ✓ A tracked shipment needs to be one of the eBay-acknowledged carriers – USPS, UPS, FedEx, and DHL are supported as the carriers.

3. ✓ The absence of a valid tracking number is liable to disputes – Buyers may open a case for "Item Not Received".

🔍 **Example**: A seller, who had two incidents in a row by not uploading tracking info/options properly, got refunds and even some negative feedback, and consequently lost their high rating among the store ranking.

Step 2: Converting AMZL Tracking to an Accepted Format

Option 1: Using BlueCare Express (BCE)

1. Log up in BlueCare Expression (In Lower BCE your destination).

2. AMZL tracking number is to be copied from your Amazon order.

3. Paste it into BCE's tool for tracking conversion to get new BCE tracking number.

4. Make eBay store updated with newly generated BCE number to see trackable shipping of the item.

🚀 **Tip**: BCE auto-syncs with eBay and provides real-time tracking updates.

Option 2: Using Third-Party Tracking Converters

1. TrackPackage & TrackingMore – Deal Ultrabox

2. ShipTrack App – Helps check and connect other tracking numbers.

📌 **Example**: A trader changed to BCE and increased their sales by 50% and disputes "Item Not Received" dropped by 50% within a month.

Step 3: Automating AMZL Tracking Conversions

1. AutoDS & Yaballe – These are the systems that I use, and I'm satisfied with BCE, which is an automated tool that tracks all of my conversions.

2. Enable Auto-Tracking – This ensures the update of tracking numbers with no need for manual work.

3. Monitor Buyer Inquiries – Track the buyers' issues related to the problems with the tracking numbers on time so as not to affect your seller ratings.

🔍 **Tip**: The time they invest automating the tracking of their orders is saved and the disputes that arise from the unavailable tracking codes are also evaded.

Conclusion: Avoid Tracking Issues, Maintain Seller Reputation

Transforming AMZL tracking numbers to eBay-compatible formats is a necessary process for the operational course maintenance of a warehouse. You can do this in different ways, you can choose either Benson Conversion Engine, or another tracking conversion tool to keep everything up to date by securing your business.

🔥 **Action Step**: Sign up with BCE or a similar service and finish off the conversion of all your pending AMZL tracking numbers.

Next up: One-Click Copy Buyer Name and Shipping Address to Amazon. 🚀

Chapter 16:
One-Click Copy Buyer Name and Shipping Address to Amazon

Why Automate Buyer Address Entry?

When one manually sends copies to Amazon by using the contact information of the eBay buyer, not only is it time-consuming, but it can also contain errors. Automating these processes with browser extensions or automation tools will help the sellers save time, avoid errors, and increase the speed of delivering orders, thus making the customers happy.

Step 1: Using Browser Extensions for One-Click Copy

1. ✅ AutoDS Buyer Info Copier – This tool has a very efficient feature that can copy all the buyer details you need to post on Amazon.

2. ✅ Yaballe Address Copier – This plug-in can be used to copy the buyer's details from the eBay website including names, shipping addresses, and phone numbers. All you need is one-click for the extension to do the rest. Just copy your customer's information on eBay and paste it in the corresponding field in Amazon.

3. ✅ DS Titan Auto-Fill – This is a great tool for Amazon. It quickly and accurately fills out the Amazon checkout fields.

🔍 **Example**: One producer took the switch to AutoDS and says it contributed to 70% faster order processing.

Step 2: Setting Up Auto-Fill for Faster Processing

1. Install the Extension – By clicking the options "Download and install AutoDS, Yaballe, or DS Titan" as your usual choice or one of all of them.

2. Log into eBay & Amazon – You need to be signed in to both platforms in order to see your activities.

3. Open the eBay Order Page – Click the extension to automatically duplicate it.

4. Go to Amazon Checkout – Find the paste button and click it to automatically fill in the buyer's details.

5. Review & Confirm – Check again the info and only then place the order.

🚀 **Tip**: People using the autofill options with the auto-fill tools are likely to slip less often and be faster in completing the transaction.

Step 3: The Entire Process is Automation

1. AutoDS Fulfillment Service – Automatically, after the eBay sale has been successfully made, puts the orders on Amazon.

2. Yaballe Auto-Ordering – Execute transactions without any manual input.

3. DS Titan Smart Orders – Synchronizes the order details as well as the updated tracking itself so that it requires no labor.

📌 **Example**: For instance, the seller managed to grow their store from 10 to 100 orders daily using Yaballe's auto-ordering feature.

Conclusion: Fasten the Order Fulfillment by the Power of Automation

One tool is the one-click copy, while another is the full automation services, both of which considerably enhance effectiveness. The buyer is happier with the shorter processing times and has better seller ratings.

🔥 **Action Step**: Install an auto-copy extension right now, and give it a trial for your next order.

Next up: Special Method for Using eBay Ads Without Wastage of Money. 🚀

Chapter 17:
Special Method to Use eBay Ads Without Losing a Penny

Why Use eBay Ads?

eBay Promoted Listings can help sellers increase their visibility and sales. Nevertheless, sellers will often set the ad rates too high or promote the wrong items, and in the end, they will be at a loss. Get unique instructions in this chapter to find out how to make eBay ads work without having to waste funds.

Step 1: Selecting the Right Products to Promote

1. ✓ Choose High-Margin Items – Promote the products where you can make at least 20% profit.

2. ✓ Avoid Low-Demand Listings – Identify and sell only items with consistent sales history.

3. ✓ Test Before Scaling – Begin with a small budget but before running ad volume, check your ROAS.

🔍 **Example**: A seller, who was promoting a popular phone case wherein he had a 25% profit margin, noted an increase of 40% in his daily sales.

Step 2: Setting Up Cost-Effective Promoted Listings

1. Go to eBay Seller Hub – Go to "The Advertising Dashboard" in seller hubs, which is part of the navigation.

2. Select Listings for Promotion – Lastly, the most desirable items will be chosen to be the ones to be promoted.

3. Set Ad Rate Strategically – Initially, bid low for 2-5% of click sale rates so you can adjust the performance based on the feedback.

4. Monitor Click-Through Rate (CTR) – Use the CTR reading to judge the productivity of the ad because you will have the data from there.

5. Refine Listings – Aside from the keyword optimizing in title and images, you can also improve your promotion by keyword-optimized navigation and search filter preferences.

📌 **Tip**: eBay suggests an ad rate, but for cost control, one may select a lower figure.

Step 3: Using Advanced Strategies to Reduce Costs

1. Promote Only Winning Products – Avoid the products that are slower in selling and focus on the newer, high-demand items.

2. Use Seasonal Trends – If high demand is expected, the ad budget can be increased, and during the high-demand season, the ad spend can be adjusted.

3. Test Different Ad Rates – Do some trials with the rates individually for each of them and decide on the one with the better ROI.

📌 **Example**: A seller decided the only shining products should be promoted and by just 30%, the ad expenses were decreased, whereas the sales increased.

Step 4: Monitoring and Adjusting for Maximum ROI

1. To measure the effectiveness of your advertising, you should collect the data that you learned during the eBay Ads Dashboard and then adjust your bid rates.

2. On a regular basis, check over the items to find the best, most attractive images and the most relevant information that users want.

3. Suspend Low-Performance Ads – Avoid advertising non-profitable products by ceasing to promote them.

🔍 **Tip**: Consistently checking ad performance not only helps you to earn more profit but also saves money.

Conclusion: Smart Ad Spending for Higher Profits

When promoting products and services, by smartly choosing products, setting the most favorable advertising rates, and monitoring results, one can make use of it effectively without losing one's hard-earned profits. By appropriately advertising the products, you minimize the negative rates and get the best results.

🔥 **Action Step**: Choose three products that you think will sell well, and then advertise them at a low rate.

Next up: Temp Payment Holds on eBay for New Sellers (Explanation). 🚀

Chapter 18:
Temp Payment Holds on eBay for New Sellers (Explanation)

Why eBay Holds Payments for New Sellers

One of the experiences that a seller might have is the possibility of a temporary payment hold when he starts selling on eBay. While this may be a common method to protect the interests of everybody, it is created for the purpose of ensuring that successful order fulfillment is done before the releasing of funds has been done.

When the seller first starts selling on eBay, he may have temporary payment holds. This is a tactic commonly used to protect and make sellers and buyers happy with the product outcome by making sure that the funds are only released when the order is fulfilled successfully and the product is received by the buyer.

When you start selling on eBay, you might be put on temporary payment holds. The institution uses this mechanism in order to insulate both the buyer and the seller.

The information one can get about the eBay payment hold policy gives the seller confidence and full knowledge to deal with such issues. PayPal Pending Payment Hold – We understand the frustration you have when payments are held. But on the other hand, you are protected as a seller when the funds are not yet released until the delivery is successful or order fulfillment has been done. If this is not the case, your money will be refunded so there is no risk. Buyers get the item only when they have made your payment. It is also necessary to have a well-maintained shipping account.

Step 1: Understanding eBay's Payment Hold Policy

✓ **eBay**, as a rule, holds payment for the first 21 days or until shipment is confirmed with a tracking note.

Step 2: How to Get Paid Faster

- **Provide Valid Tracking** – As the order gets shipped, provide tracking information immediately.

- **Mark Orders as Shipped** – Verify with eBay once you have shipped the package in their system.

- **Deliver Great Customer Service** – If the buyers give positive feedback, the hold removal process will be adjusted quickly.

- **Maintain a Good Seller Rating** – There should not be any disputes and late shipments to avoid reducing your seller rating.

🚀 **Tip**: Make payments faster by choosing suppliers with short shipping times (e.g., Amazon Prime, Walmart+).

Step 3: Transitioning to Instant Payments

- **Sell Regularly** – Consistent sales activity helps you to become a good seller and minimize the hold of your funds.

- **Build Positive Feedback** – A higher feedback score is a sign of trust.

- **Meet eBay's Seller Performance Standards** – Contracting above the standard level will help to save you from the restrictions.

📌 **Example**: A seller with a 98% positive rating who uploaded tracking on time had his holds lifted in 60 days only.

Conclusion: Overcoming Payment Holds Efficiently

Their temporary holds are annoying, but we still have to face them. The best way to mitigate hold times and get to your funds is to process your orders swiftly, perform well as a seller, and obey eBay's regulations.

🔥 **Action Step**: Ship out the orders on time and try to gather positive reviews from buyers so that your credibility level goes up.

Next up: **Customer Service #1 - How to Find Solutions for Client Questions (Q&A).** 🚀

Chapter 19:
Customer Service #1 – How to Find Solutions for Client Questions (Q&A)

Why Excellent Customer Service Matters

Good customer service brings customer satisfaction and trust, is helpful in handling conflicts, and reduces problems. Satisfying customer inquiries with appropriate formulation in real time and high accuracy are likely to yield a high level of sales and a well-established group of loyal customers.

Step 1: Common Buyer Questions and How to Handle Them

✓ **"When will my order arrive?"** – See the details from the tracking and give an estimated delivery date.

✓ **"Can I cancel my order?"** – If the item has not been shipped, allow for a cancellation; if the item is shipped, give instructions on the recovery process.

✓ **"Do you offer refunds?"** – Bring customers to the return policy through your website and guide them on how to process a return.

✓ **"Is this item authentic?"** – Reassure buyers with a well-communicated written product description and images that are of high quality.

🔍 **Example**: A seller who answered inquiries within one hour registered the highest positive feedback increase - 20%.

Step 2: Use eBay's Messaging System Properly

- **Turn on Automated Responses** – Make sure you have the necessary information in the master.

- **Check This Site Every Day** – Buyers will leave you feedback within 24 hours.

- **Be Professional and Polite** – Be nice to other people, even if they act bad to you.

- **Deal With Situations Timely** – Present ideas that help to prevent disputes and positive feedback.

🚀 **Tip**: Fast clear-text responses are key to improving your eBay seller rating and your buyer confidence.

Step 3: Leveraging FAQs to Minimize Repetitive Questions

- **Update Product Descriptions** – Address the major concerns of the buyers in advance.

- **Use an FAQ Section in Listings** – Reply to the buyers' questions which are more often than those they have actually asked.

- **Provide Clear Return & Shipping Policies** – Save your time from answering the questions that the customers can find in the return and shipping policies.

📌 **Example**: A seller increased the visibility of the FAQs by adding them to the listings and saw a 30% reduction in customer inquiries.

Conclusion: How to be a Customer Service Pro

Being there for surgical new england meeting by giving prompt and accurate answers is a way to ensure customer satisfaction and is a foundation for business development in the long run. Employing such an approach reduces complaints and brings back the old customers.

● **Action Step**: Implement automated responses to buyers' three most common questions as soon as possible.

Next up: **Customer Service #2 - How to Handle Product Returns and Get Shipping Labels from Amazon.**

Chapter 20:
Customer Service #2 – How to Handle Product Returns and Get Shipping Labels from Amazon

Why Handling Returns Efficiently is Important

Keeping returns in check is not only good for your seller reputation but also leads to lower negative feedback and better customer satisfaction. The return procedure that runs without hiccups promotes buyer-seller trust.

Step 1: Understanding eBay's Return Policies

✓ **30-Day Returns (Preferred)** – Providing free returns is a trustworthy approach to do so and it will also get you to the top of the search result.

✓ **Buyer Pays for Return Shipping** – This type is common among gadgets and it really helps with that.

✓ **No Returns Policy** – Regarding the No-Return-Policy, it is mostly a bad idea as you risk losing the sale by not having such an option.

🔍 **Example**: A seller that volunteered free 30-day returns, among other enhancements, noticed a 12% increase in second iterations of faithfulness.

Step 2: Processing a Return Request on eBay

- **Go to eBay Seller Hub** – Click the 'Return' button to be transferred to a separate page.
- **Approve the Return** – If you are, go ahead and say "Yes" to the request from the buyer.

- **Provide a Return Label** – The customers can return the items they do not like and receive their money back.

- **Issue a Refund** – Once we get the items and check them, we will send a refund.

The key herein is to give fast responses to claims so as to avoid disputes and chargebacks.

Step 3: Getting a Return Label from Amazon

- **Log in to Your Amazon Account** – Already signed in? Click on the "Account" link, and then hover over "Orders > Manage Orders."

- **Find the Item** – Click Replace Items, or you can also return the item to the seller.

- **Select the Reason** – Choose the 'Do not need the product anymore.'

- **Download the Prepaid Label** – The products in the Amazon store can be labeled as to whether they are available for download.

- **Send the Label to the Buyer** – After that, send him the label by using eBay's return system or by e-mailing it to him.

📌 **Example**: A seller that gave return labels as an initiative only saw a dispute reduction of 40%.

Step 4: Handling Refunds Correctly

- **Refunds Timely** – The item should be refunded in the next 48 hours, no later than that.

- **Examine the Product's Condition** – Be sure the product is in its original state before you issue a refund.

- **Lose Points in the Restocking Category (If It is Apply)** – Was possible only for particular categories.

🔍 **Tip**: Gathering and keeping records of the returns will decrease the number of cases with irregular claims.

Conclusion: Streamline Your Return Process

By managing returns well, users feel stronger faith in your product and there is no dispute left for them to pass through. Use Amazon's return labels and follow eBay's rules and regulations, and you will, in return, offer hassle-free service to both you and the buyer.

🔥 **Action Step**: Process an open dry run request and revise your return policy for the better.

Finally: **Final Thoughts & Scaling Your eBay Dropshipping Business.** 🚀

Final Thoughts & Scaling Your eBay Dropshipping Business

Reflecting on Your Dropshipping Journey

Congratulations! You've gone through all the absolutely necessary procedures of starting and running an eBay dropshipping business. Already you have an understanding of product sourcing, QR code technology, and acquaintance of customer service. Moreover, you have acquired the movie-like skill of handling returns quickly. Although, the getting-the-hang-of-things stage is merely an introduction to the business of size. Scaling is the ability to increase the business systematically while keeping profitability and efficiency. This piece is to provide you with the necessary steps to diversify the list of your products, streamline operations, launch and scale a new product line, and globalize your business. If you apply the right technique, you may become a steady source of income through the eBay extravaganza.

Step 1: Expanding Your Product Listings

The better, more products you list, the more chance of your selling will be. However, if you don't list products in a systematic way, the likelihood of you being successful will decrease. You must make your decision on which product to choose using numbers and facts.

Finding High-Demand Products

1. **Use Product Research Tools** – Websites such as Zik Analytics and AutoDS are beneficial for finding out which are the most popular and profitable products.

2. **Analyze eBay's Best Sellers** – Visit eBay's trending section and take a look at what items in your niche are selling high.

3. **Check Competitor Listings** – Examine good sellers in your category and determine which ones are the most purchased.

🔍 **Example**: John, a dropshipper, used Zik Analytics to determine what products were hot-sellers during his flexible hours. He would sell 50 more products and grow by 60% over just 3 months.

Optimizing Existing Listings for More Sales

- **Revise titles for better SEO** – Incorporate top-qualifying keywords.

- **Improve product images** – A good visual representation will lure consumers.

- **Enhance descriptions** – Be specific about the product benefits and real shipping details.

🚀 **Tip**: The listings that get better rankings in search results are more visible, thus increasing sales. Always, update and optimize opposed listings to keep them appealing.

Step 2: Automating Your Operations

Doing the work of managing a large number of listings and purchasing orders manually can be a very onerous task. Automating is the key to the scaling without burning out.

Essential Automation Tools

- **AutoDS & Yaballe** – Automate product sourcing, repricing, and order placement.

- **EcomDash & Inventory Source** – Keep track of your inventory and avoid overstocking situations.

- **Zendesk & Freshdesk** – Automatically replace calls to simple questions using your bot and template in Zendesk and Freshdesk, respectively.

How to Implement Automation Step-by-Step

1. **Set Up Auto-Ordering** – Let AutoDS do the buying for you when an item goes away.

2. **Enable Price Monitoring** – Set default settings and price course based on their edged source.

3. **Create Auto-Responses** – Generate canned responses for the most common customers' inquiries.

📌 **Example**: Taking a cue from a pro like Sarah, who has been selling stuff like a bird for years, she got a relief from the workload stress by 75% when she incorporated automation tools of AutoDS, which eventually have her focused on scaling.

🚀 **Tip**: With automation, the more time you spend on strategic business growth, the more likely you are to excel at it.

Step 3: Increasing Your eBay Selling Limits

At the beginning, eBay has limited the number of products you can sell every month. If you want to grow, you have to request the increased limits.

How to Request a Selling Limit Increase

1. **Go to eBay Seller Hub** – Click on the "Request Limit Increase" part of the section to get to the page.

2. **Be a Perfect Vendor** – Take care of the customers' positive feedback and fewer order errors.

3. **Contact eBay Support** – Be humble in asking for a higher limit and give the reason for you wanting it

✓ **Additional Ways to Increase Limits:**

- Make customer satisfaction ratings higher.
- Sell continuously for three months as the minimum.
- Show evidence for inventory sources only if required by sellers.

🔍 **Example**: Mark is a perfect illustration of a person who skillfully achieved as such; he is the one who switched his selling limits from only 10 items a month to 1,000 items in just six months!

🚀 **Tip**: The online selling platform would rather compliance demonstration in approving your request than taking chances.

Step 4: Expanding to Other Marketplaces

Set up a rewarding market at your eBay store and think of further platforms for falling back on your profits that come from different sources.

Best Marketplaces for Dropshipping Expansion

- **Walmart Marketplace** – Currently faced with minimum competition and with rising numbers of shoppers.

- **Facebook Marketplace** – Not charged for listing and is fitting for local trading.

- **Etsy (for Handmade & Vintage Items)** – It's good for niche items or those that are easily personalizable which are usually the customer's choices.

- **Amazon FBA** – Check on the availability of Amazon FBA services if you want to implement delivery by this worldwide leader of e-commerce company.

How to Expand Successfully

1. **Recreate Your eBay Links** – Go to some well-performing goods records on other platforms for example.

2. **Adhere to Site Regulations** – You can find the same rules on different platforms but in case of doubt, read and abide by them.

3. **Track Progress** – Observe sales data so as to convince which are the most popular products.

📌 **Example**: In an instance involving one of the sellers who expanded to this channel, we have evidence that he added $5,000 each month more to his revenue as fast as within only three months.

🔍 **Tip**: The most effective way of optimizing your platform(s) is the strategy of diversifying on various platforms in order to free yourself from being so tightly bound to eBay and to increase total sales in general.

Step 5: Investing in Branding & Long-Term Growth

Expanding the brand may be the key to your success thus you should consider giving it a special touch to make it outstanding from your competitors.

Branding Strategies for Dropshippers

1. **Create a Shopify Store** – Start the brand from scratch outside of the marketplaces.

2. **Use Custom Packaging** – Most suppliers will do the branding for you.

3. **Develop Social Media Presence** – The more community you create, the more for sure people will repetitively shop from you.

📌 **Example**: For instance, one someone who had OnceDecided and WokeUpTo theNOWturff saw the difference between selling a playground on eBay and selling via a linked spot-on Shopify page, the first being the less profitable one in the end.

🚀 **Tip**: Branding allows you to not just tie the customer once but to bring them back later boosting the lifetime value.

Final Words: Take Action & Keep Scaling

Dropshipping on eBay is an excellent source of income with less investment. Remember that the critical actions taken will be the consistency, process optimization, and strategy for the deal to move in the right direction. Being in the beginning stage of creation or being ready to scale, the sky is the limit.

Your Next Steps:

- 🔥 **Set a goal** – Double your current sales volume in the next three months.

- 🔥 **Implement automation** – Eliminate manual tasks to focus on the growth of your business.

- 🔥 **Expand wisely** – Try new marketplaces to add more income sources.

Success is a process of learning and adjusting. Be one step ahead in your business by keeping up with new trends, adjusting your approach, and especially by doing something today!

Good luck and in the name of sales celebrate like a pro!

Thank you for reading!

We believe that you have found the confidence and the right tools to start off as a prosperous vendor on eBay from this manual. The fear of starting something fresh is common as it makes one feel like there are so many things which are not known but with some tips & determination one can go about it.

In case you found this book useful, here's another great resource for increasing your income and discovering flexible employment options:

100+ PROVEN WAYS TO MAKE MONEY FROM HOME

DISCOVER HOW TO MAKE $200/HOUR

Work From Home Jobs, Passive Income Ideas, Freelance, Full/Part-Time, Side Hustle Opportunities For Beginners And Experts

CLICK HERE TO GET YOUR COPY NOW!

OR SCAN THE QR CODE

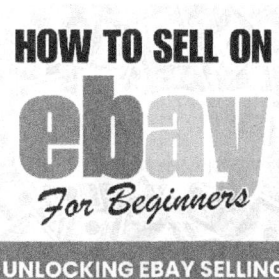

If you want tips that you can easily use to get real online home jobs, then this is the book for you. It does not matter if you are in search of extra cash, beginning a full-time job far from the office, or considering freelancing – this book will be essential for all of those cases!

In this course you will learn about:

- ✓ Tips for Recognizing Profitable Remote Jobs Relevant to Your Skill Set
- ✓ Leading sectors that employ freelancers as well as remote workers
- ✓ Advice on how to get a job on the Internet for beginners
- ✓ Instruments & sources to maximize income

Why would you be satisfied with one source of income when you could access several sources without leaving your home?

Start your journey toward financial freedom today!

In case it supports you, remember leaving behind some feedback after reading this book. By leaving your feedback, you will be able to help other people see that there are some good resources that can be found here & also support the author.

We appreciate having you in our community of motivated learners & entrepreneurs. We wish you all the best as you continue to progress!